I'VE Totally got This

MOOD TRACKER JOURNAL

DAY: M T W T F S S 🦋 DATE _____

(Mood Tracker)

Morning:

Afternoon:

Evening:

Other:

Was both frustrated & tired
by the evening.

Three words To Describe Today:

1) Stressful.

2) Exhausting.

3) frustrating..

🦋 🦋 🦋 🦋 🦋 🦋 🦋

One thing I'm grateful for is: My friend Cathy

What could have improved today? If I had gone for the run I'd
planned on first thing this morning.

Three Goals For Tomorrow:

1) Do a 5k run

2) Call my friend Cathy

3) Sort out my clothes - sort stuff to se___

🦋 🦋 🦋 🦋 🦋 🦋

B Banana and porridge. Te___

L Gluten free tuna sandwich berries, 2 bits chocolate.

D Chicken & sweet potato curry. Rice. Mango chutney. water.

S For a snack - I just had some toast and peanut butter.

ENERGY LEVELS:

Morning: 8 /10   Afternoon: 6 /10   Evening: 2 /10

Exercise: Y/(N) Details/Activity:
I was meant to run but I didn't.... I had a short walk,
about 20 min to the store. But still the fresh air helped!

The BEST part of the day was.....
I actually had a nice chat with my dad this evening, which helped calm
me a bit before bed and feel less frustrated..

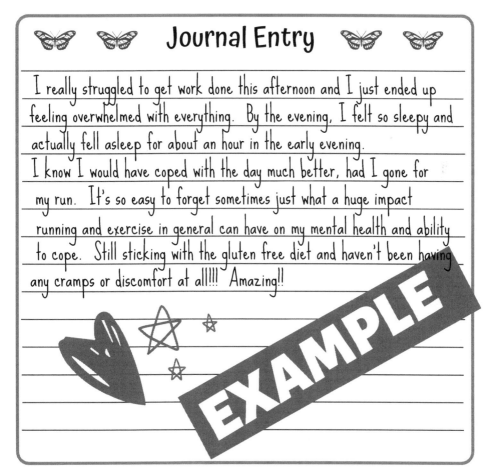

Journal Entry

I really struggled to get work done this afternoon and I just ended up
feeling overwhelmed with everything. By the evening, I felt so sleepy and
actually fell asleep for about an hour in the early evening.
I know I would have coped with the day much better, had I gone for
my run. It's so easy to forget sometimes just what a huge impact
running and exercise in general can have on my mental health and ability
to cope. Still sticking with the gluten free diet and haven't been having
any cramps or discomfort at all!!! Amazing!!

DAY: M T W T F S S 🦋 DATE 2/1/2022

(Mood Tracker)

Morning:

Afternoon:

Evening:

Other:

Three words To Describe Today:

1)_____

2)_____

3)_____

🦋 🦋 🦋 🦋 🦋 🦋 🦋

One thing I'm grateful for is:_____

What could have improved today?_____

_____

Three Goals For Tomorrow:

1)_____

2)_____

3)_____

🦋 🦋 🦋 Meals & Snacks 🦋 🦋 🦋

B_____

L_____

D_____

S_____

ENERGY LEVELS:

Morning: 3 /10   Afternoon: /10   Evening: /10

Exercise: Y/N   Details/Activity:

The BEST part of the day was.....

_____

_____

_____

Journal Entry

_____

_____

_____

_____

_____

_____

_____

_____

_____

_____

_____

_____

_____

_____

DAY: M T W T F S S   DATE_____

(Mood Tracker)

Morning:

Afternoon:

Evening:

Other:

Three words To Describe Today:

1)_____

2)_____

3)_____

One thing I'm grateful for is:_____

What could have improved today?_____

_____

Three Goals For Tomorrow:

1)_____

2)_____

3)_____

Meals & Snacks

B_____

L_____

D_____

S_____

ENERGY LEVELS:

Morning: /10   Afternoon: /10   Evening: /10

Exercise: Y/N   Details/Activity:

The BEST part of the day was.....

_____

_____

_____

Journal Entry

_____

_____

_____

_____

_____

_____

_____

_____

_____

_____

_____

_____

_____

_____

_____

DAY: M T W T F S S 🦋 DATE _____

(Mood Tracker)

Morning:

Afternoon:

Evening:

Other:

Three words To Describe Today:

1) _____

2) _____

3) _____

🦋   🦋   🦋   🦋   🦋   🦋   🦋

One thing I'm grateful for is: _____

What could have improved today? _____

_____

Three Goals For Tomorrow:

1) _____

2) _____

3) _____

🦋   🦋   🦋   Meals & Snacks   🦋   🦋   🦋

B _____

L _____

D _____

S _____

ENERGY LEVELS:

Morning: /10   Afternoon: /10   Evening: /10

Exercise: Y/N   Details/Activity:

The BEST part of the day was.....

_____

_____

_____

Journal Entry

_____

_____

_____

_____

_____

_____

_____

_____

_____

_____

_____

_____

_____

_____

DAY: M T W T F S S   DATE _____

(Mood Tracker)

Morning:

Afternoon:

Evening:

Other:

Three words To Describe Today:

1) _____

2) _____

3) _____

One thing I'm grateful for is: _____

What could have improved today? _____

_____

Three Goals For Tomorrow:

1) _____

2) _____

3) _____

Meals & Snacks

B _____

L _____

D _____

S _____

ENERGY LEVELS:

Morning: /10   Afternoon: /10   Evening: /10

Exercise: Y/N   Details/Activity:

The BEST part of the day was.....

_____

_____

_____

Journal Entry

_____

_____

_____

_____

_____

_____

_____

_____

_____

_____

_____

_____

_____

DAY: M T W T F S S   DATE _____

(Mood Tracker)

Morning: Afternoon:

Evening: Other:

Three words To Describe Today:

1) _____

2) _____

3) _____

One thing I'm grateful for is: _____

What could have improved today? _____

_____

Three Goals For Tomorrow:

1) _____

2) _____

3) _____

Meals & Snacks

B _____

L _____

D _____

S _____

ENERGY LEVELS:

Morning: /10   Afternoon: /10   Evening: /10

Exercise: Y/N   Details/Activity:

The BEST part of the day was.....

_____

_____

_____

Journal Entry

_____

_____

_____

_____

_____

_____

_____

_____

_____

_____

_____

_____

_____

_____

_____

DAY: M T W T F S S 🦋 DATE _____

(Mood Tracker)

Morning: Afternoon:

Evening: Other:

Three words To Describe Today:

1) _____

2) _____

3) _____

🦋 🦋 🦋 🦋 🦋 🦋 🦋

One thing I'm grateful for is: _____

What could have improved today? _____

_____

Three Goals For Tomorrow:

1) _____

2) _____

3) _____

🦋 🦋 🦋 Meals & Snacks 🦋 🦋 🦋

B _____

L _____

D _____

S _____

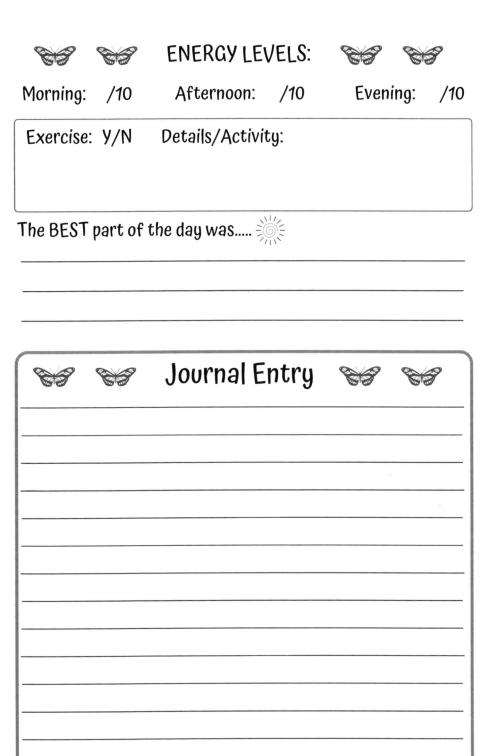

ENERGY LEVELS:

Morning: /10   Afternoon: /10   Evening: /10

Exercise: Y/N   Details/Activity:

The BEST part of the day was.....

_____

_____

_____

Journal Entry

_____

_____

_____

_____

_____

_____

_____

_____

_____

_____

_____

_____

_____

_____

_____

DAY: M T W T F S S 🦋 DATE_____

(Mood Tracker)

Morning:

Afternoon:

Evening:

Other:

Three words To Describe Today:

1)_____

2)_____

3)_____

One thing I'm grateful for is:_____

What could have improved today?_____

_____

Three Goals For Tomorrow:

1)_____

2)_____

3)_____

Meals & Snacks

B_____

L_____

D_____

S_____

🦋 🦋 ENERGY LEVELS: 🦋 🦋

Morning: /10   Afternoon: /10   Evening: /10

Exercise: Y/N   Details/Activity:

The BEST part of the day was..... ☼

_____

_____

_____

Journal Entry 🦋 🦋

_____

_____

_____

_____

_____

_____

_____

_____

_____

_____

_____

_____

_____

_____

DAY: M T W T F S S DATE _____

(Mood Tracker)

Morning:

Afternoon:

Evening:

Other:

Three words To Describe Today:

1) _____

2) _____

3) _____

One thing I'm grateful for is: _____

What could have improved today? _____

_____

Three Goals For Tomorrow:

1) _____

2) _____

3) _____

Meals & Snacks

B _____

L _____

D _____

S _____

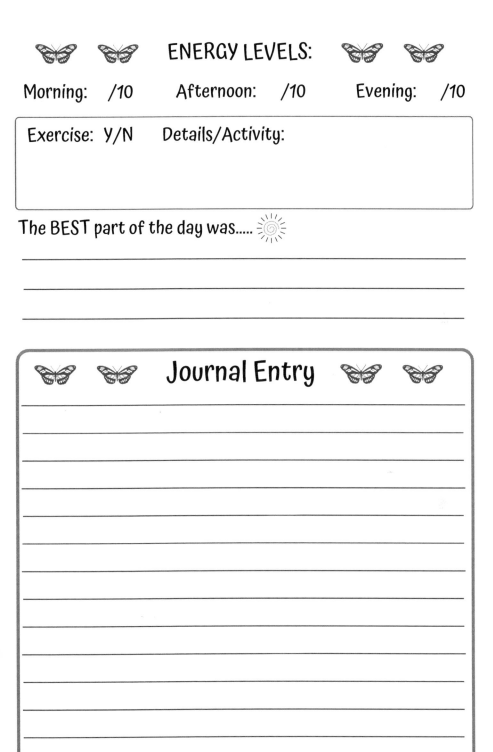

ENERGY LEVELS:

Morning: /10   Afternoon: /10   Evening: /10

Exercise: Y/N   Details/Activity:

The BEST part of the day was.....

_____

_____

_____

Journal Entry

_____

_____

_____

_____

_____

_____

_____

_____

_____

_____

_____

_____

_____

_____

_____

_____

DAY: M T W T F S S 🦋 DATE_____

(Mood Tracker)

Morning:

Afternoon:

Evening:

Other:

Three words To Describe Today:

1)_____

2)_____

3)_____

One thing I'm grateful for is:_____

What could have improved today?_____

_____

Three Goals For Tomorrow:

1)_____

2)_____

3)_____

Meals & Snacks

B_____

L_____

D_____

S_____

ENERGY LEVELS:

Morning: /10   Afternoon: /10   Evening: /10

Exercise: Y/N   Details/Activity:

The BEST part of the day was.....

_____

_____

_____

Journal Entry

_____

_____

_____

_____

_____

_____

_____

_____

_____

_____

_____

_____

_____

_____

_____

_____

DAY: M T W T F S S 🦋 DATE_____

(Mood Tracker)

Morning:

Afternoon:

Evening:

Other:

Three words To Describe Today:

1)_____

2)_____

3)_____

One thing I'm grateful for is:_____

What could have improved today?_____

_____

Three Goals For Tomorrow:

1)_____

2)_____

3)_____

Meals & Snacks

B_____

L_____

D_____

S_____

ENERGY LEVELS:

Morning: /10   Afternoon: /10   Evening: /10

Exercise: Y/N   Details/Activity:

The BEST part of the day was.....

_____

_____

_____

Journal Entry

_____

_____

_____

_____

_____

_____

_____

_____

_____

_____

_____

_____

_____

_____

_____

DAY: M T W T F S S 🦋 DATE_____

(Mood Tracker)

Morning:

Afternoon:

Evening:

Other:

Three words To Describe Today:

1)_____

2)_____

3)_____

🦋　　🦋　　🦋　　🦋　　🦋　　🦋　　🦋

One thing I'm grateful for is:_____

What could have improved today?_____

_____

Three Goals For Tomorrow:

1)_____

2)_____

3)_____

🦋　　🦋　　🦋　　Meals & Snacks　　🦋　　🦋　　🦋

B_____

L_____

D_____

S_____

ENERGY LEVELS:

Morning: /10   Afternoon: /10   Evening: /10

Exercise: Y/N   Details/Activity:

The BEST part of the day was.....

_____

_____

_____

Journal Entry

_____

_____

_____

_____

_____

_____

_____

_____

_____

_____

_____

_____

_____

_____

_____

DAY: M T W T F S S   DATE _____

(Mood Tracker)

Morning:

Afternoon:

Evening:

Other:

Three words To Describe Today:

1) _____
2) _____
3) _____

One thing I'm grateful for is: _____

What could have improved today? _____

_____

Three Goals For Tomorrow:

1) _____
2) _____
3) _____

Meals & Snacks

B _____
L _____
D _____
S _____

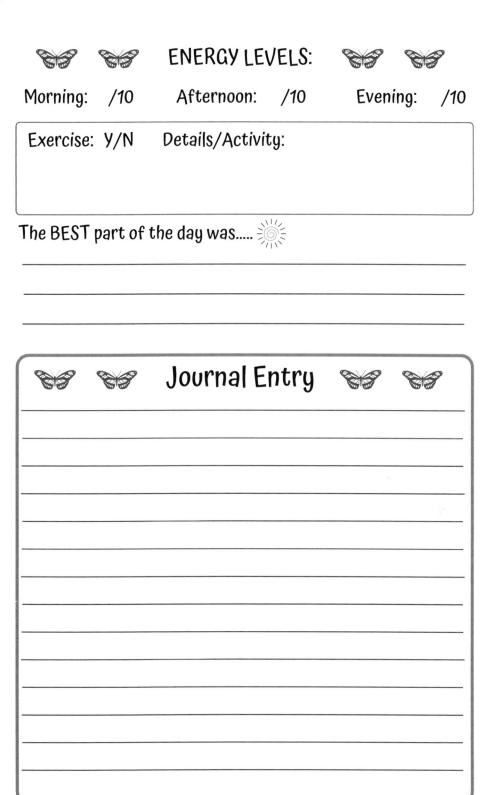

ENERGY LEVELS:

Morning: /10   Afternoon: /10   Evening: /10

Exercise: Y/N   Details/Activity:

The BEST part of the day was.....

_____

_____

_____

Journal Entry

_____

_____

_____

_____

_____

_____

_____

_____

_____

_____

_____

_____

_____

_____

DAY: M T W T F S S   DATE_____

(Mood Tracker)

Morning:

Afternoon:

Evening:

Other:

Three words To Describe Today:

1)_____

2)_____

3)_____

One thing I'm grateful for is:_____

What could have improved today?_____

_____

Three Goals For Tomorrow:

1)_____

2)_____

3)_____

Meals & Snacks

B_____

L_____

D_____

S_____

ENERGY LEVELS:

Morning: /10   Afternoon: /10   Evening: /10

Exercise: Y/N   Details/Activity:

The BEST part of the day was..... ☀

_____

_____

_____

Journal Entry

_____

_____

_____

_____

_____

_____

_____

_____

_____

_____

_____

_____

_____

_____

_____

DAY: M T W T F S S 🦋 DATE_____

(Mood Tracker)

Morning:

Afternoon:

Evening:

Other:

Three words To Describe Today:

1)_____

2)_____

3)_____

🦋　　🦋　　🦋　　🦋　　🦋　　🦋　　🦋

One thing I'm grateful for is:_____

What could have improved today?_____

_____

Three Goals For Tomorrow:

1)_____

2)_____

3)_____

🦋　　🦋　　🦋　　Meals & Snacks　　🦋　　🦋　　🦋

B_____

L_____

D_____

S_____

ENERGY LEVELS:

Morning: /10   Afternoon: /10   Evening: /10

Exercise: Y/N   Details/Activity:

The BEST part of the day was.....

_____

_____

_____

Journal Entry

_____

_____

_____

_____

_____

_____

_____

_____

_____

_____

_____

_____

_____

DAY: M T W T F S S ☐ DATE_____

(Mood Tracker)

Morning:

Afternoon:

Evening:

Other:

Three words To Describe Today:

1)_____
2)_____
3)_____

One thing I'm grateful for is:_____

What could have improved today?_____

_____

Three Goals For Tomorrow:

1)_____
2)_____
3)_____

Meals & Snacks

B_____
L_____
D_____
S_____

ENERGY LEVELS:

Morning: /10   Afternoon: /10   Evening: /10

Exercise: Y/N   Details/Activity:

The BEST part of the day was..... ☀

_____

_____

_____

Journal Entry

_____
_____
_____
_____
_____
_____
_____
_____
_____
_____
_____
_____
_____
_____
_____

DAY: M T W T F S S DATE _____

(Mood Tracker)

Morning:

Afternoon:

Evening:

Other:

Three words To Describe Today:

1) _____

2) _____

3) _____

One thing I'm grateful for is: _____

What could have improved today? _____

_____

Three Goals For Tomorrow:

1) _____

2) _____

3) _____

Meals & Snacks

B _____

L _____

D _____

S _____

ENERGY LEVELS:

Morning: /10   Afternoon: /10   Evening: /10

Exercise: Y/N   Details/Activity:

The BEST part of the day was.....

_____

_____

_____

Journal Entry

_____

_____

_____

_____

_____

_____

_____

_____

_____

_____

_____

_____

_____

_____

_____

DAY: M T W T F S S 🦋 DATE_____

(Mood Tracker)

Morning:

Afternoon:

Evening:

Other:

Three words To Describe Today:

1)_____

2)_____

3)_____

🦋 🦋 🦋 🦋 🦋 🦋 🦋

One thing I'm grateful for is:_____

What could have improved today?_____

_____

Three Goals For Tomorrow:

1)_____

2)_____

3)_____

🦋   🦋   🦋   Meals & Snacks   🦋   🦋   🦋

B_____

L_____

D_____

S_____

ENERGY LEVELS:

Morning: /10   Afternoon: /10   Evening: /10

Exercise: Y/N   Details/Activity:

The BEST part of the day was.....

_____

_____

_____

Journal Entry

_____

_____

_____

_____

_____

_____

_____

_____

_____

_____

_____

_____

_____

_____

_____

DAY: M T W T F S S DATE_____

(Mood Tracker)

Morning:

Afternoon:

Evening:

Other:

Three words To Describe Today:

1)_____

2)_____

3)_____

One thing I'm grateful for is:_____

What could have improved today?_____

_____

Three Goals For Tomorrow:

1)_____

2)_____

3)_____

Meals & Snacks

B_____

L_____

D_____

S_____

ENERGY LEVELS:

Morning: /10   Afternoon: /10   Evening: /10

Exercise: Y/N   Details/Activity:

The BEST part of the day was.....

_____

_____

_____

Journal Entry

_____

_____

_____

_____

_____

_____

_____

_____

_____

_____

_____

_____

_____

_____

_____

DAY: M T W T F S S 🦋 DATE_____

(Mood Tracker)

Morning:

Afternoon:

Evening:

Other:

Three words To Describe Today:

1)_____

2)_____

3)_____

One thing I'm grateful for is:_____

What could have improved today?_____

_____

Three Goals For Tomorrow:

1)_____

2)_____

3)_____

Meals & Snacks

B_____

L_____

D_____

S_____

ENERGY LEVELS:

Morning: /10   Afternoon: /10   Evening: /10

Exercise: Y/N   Details/Activity:

The BEST part of the day was.....

_____

_____

_____

Journal Entry

_____

_____

_____

_____

_____

_____

_____

_____

_____

_____

_____

_____

_____

_____

DAY: M T W T F S S 🦋 DATE _____

(Mood Tracker)

Morning:

Afternoon:

Evening:

Other:

Three words To Describe Today:

1) _____
2) _____
3) _____

🦋　🦋　🦋　🦋　🦋　🦋　🦋

One thing I'm grateful for is: _____

What could have improved today? _____

_____

Three Goals For Tomorrow:

1) _____
2) _____
3) _____

🦋　🦋　🦋　Meals & Snacks　🦋　🦋　🦋

B _____
L _____
D _____
S _____

ENERGY LEVELS:

Morning: /10   Afternoon: /10   Evening: /10

Exercise: Y/N   Details/Activity:

The BEST part of the day was.....

_____

_____

_____

Journal Entry

_____

_____

_____

_____

_____

_____

_____

_____

_____

_____

_____

_____

_____

_____

DAY: M T W T F S S 🦋 DATE_____

(Mood Tracker)

Morning:

Afternoon:

Evening:

Other:

Three words To Describe Today:

1)_____

2)_____

3)_____

🦋 🦋 🦋 🦋 🦋 🦋 🦋

One thing I'm grateful for is:_____

What could have improved today?_____

_____

Three Goals For Tomorrow:

1)_____

2)_____

3)_____

🦋 🦋 🦋 Meals & Snacks 🦋 🦋 🦋

B_____

L_____

D_____

S_____

ENERGY LEVELS:

Morning: /10   Afternoon: /10   Evening: /10

Exercise: Y/N   Details/Activity:

The BEST part of the day was.....

_____

_____

_____

Journal Entry

_____

_____

_____

_____

_____

_____

_____

_____

_____

_____

_____

_____

_____

_____

DAY: M T W T F S S   DATE_____

(Mood Tracker)

Morning:

Afternoon:

Evening:

Other:

Three words To Describe Today:

1)_____

2)_____

3)_____

One thing I'm grateful for is:_____

What could have improved today?_____

_____

Three Goals For Tomorrow:

1)_____

2)_____

3)_____

Meals & Snacks

B_____

L_____

D_____

S_____

ENERGY LEVELS:

Morning: /10   Afternoon: /10   Evening: /10

Exercise: Y/N   Details/Activity:

The BEST part of the day was.....

_____

_____

_____

Journal Entry

_____
_____
_____
_____
_____
_____
_____
_____
_____
_____
_____
_____
_____
_____
_____
_____

DAY: M T W T F S S 🦋 DATE_____

(Mood Tracker)

Morning: 😠 😀 😫 😨 😴

Afternoon: 😠 😀 😫 😨 😴

Evening: 😠 😀 😫 😨 😴

Other:

Three words To Describe Today:

1)_____

2)_____

3)_____

🦋 🦋 🦋 🦋 🦋 🦋 🦋

One thing I'm grateful for is:_____

What could have improved today?_____

_____

Three Goals For Tomorrow:

1)_____

2)_____

3)_____

🦋 🦋 🦋 Meals & Snacks 🦋 🦋 🦋

B_____

L_____

D_____

S_____

ENERGY LEVELS:

Morning: /10   Afternoon: /10   Evening: /10

Exercise: Y/N   Details/Activity:

The BEST part of the day was.....

_____

_____

_____

Journal Entry

_____

_____

_____

_____

_____

_____

_____

_____

_____

_____

_____

_____

_____

_____

_____

DAY: M T W T F S S 🦋 DATE_____

(Mood Tracker)

Morning:

Afternoon:

Evening:

Other:

Three words To Describe Today:

1)_____

2)_____

3)_____

🦋 🦋 🦋 🦋 🦋 🦋 🦋

One thing I'm grateful for is:_____

What could have improved today?_____

_____

Three Goals For Tomorrow:

1)_____

2)_____

3)_____

🦋 🦋 🦋 Meals & Snacks 🦋 🦋 🦋

B_____

L_____

D_____

S_____

ENERGY LEVELS:

Morning: /10   Afternoon: /10   Evening: /10

Exercise: Y/N   Details/Activity:

The BEST part of the day was.....

_____

_____

_____

Journal Entry

_____

_____

_____

_____

_____

_____

_____

_____

_____

_____

_____

_____

_____

_____

DAY: M T W T F S S DATE_____

(Mood Tracker)

Morning:

Afternoon:

Evening:

Other:

Three words To Describe Today:

1)_____

2)_____

3)_____

One thing I'm grateful for is:_____

What could have improved today?_____

_____

Three Goals For Tomorrow:

1)_____

2)_____

3)_____

Meals & Snacks

B_____

L_____

D_____

S_____

ENERGY LEVELS:

Morning: /10   Afternoon: /10   Evening: /10

Exercise: Y/N   Details/Activity:

The BEST part of the day was.....

_____

_____

_____

Journal Entry

_____

_____

_____

_____

_____

_____

_____

_____

_____

_____

_____

_____

_____

_____

_____

DAY: M T W T F S S 🦋 DATE _____

(Mood Tracker)

Morning:

Afternoon:

Evening:

Other:

Three words To Describe Today:

1)_____

2)_____

3)_____

One thing I'm grateful for is: _____

What could have improved today? _____

_____

Three Goals For Tomorrow:

1)_____

2)_____

3)_____

Meals & Snacks

B_____

L_____

D_____

S_____

ENERGY LEVELS:

Morning: /10   Afternoon: /10   Evening: /10

Exercise: Y/N   Details/Activity:

The BEST part of the day was.....

_____

_____

_____

Journal Entry

_____

_____

_____

_____

_____

_____

_____

_____

_____

_____

_____

_____

_____

_____

_____

DAY: M T W T F S S 🦋 DATE_____

(Mood Tracker)

Morning:

Afternoon:

Evening:

Other:

Three words To Describe Today:

1)_____

2)_____

3)_____

🦋 🦋 🦋 🦋 🦋 🦋 🦋

One thing I'm grateful for is:_____

What could have improved today?_____

_____

Three Goals For Tomorrow:

1)_____

2)_____

3)_____

🦋 🦋 🦋 Meals & Snacks 🦋 🦋 🦋

B_____

L_____

D_____

S_____

ENERGY LEVELS:

Morning: /10   Afternoon: /10   Evening: /10

Exercise: Y/N   Details/Activity:

The BEST part of the day was.....

_____
_____
_____

Journal Entry

_____
_____
_____
_____
_____
_____
_____
_____
_____
_____
_____
_____
_____
_____
_____

DAY: M T W T F S S 🦋 DATE_____

(Mood Tracker)

Morning:

Afternoon:

Evening:

Other:

Three words To Describe Today:

1)_____

2)_____

3)_____

🦋 🦋 🦋 🦋 🦋 🦋 🦋

One thing I'm grateful for is:_____

What could have improved today?_____

_____

Three Goals For Tomorrow:

1)_____

2)_____

3)_____

🦋 🦋 🦋 Meals & Snacks 🦋 🦋 🦋

B _____

L _____

D _____

S _____

ENERGY LEVELS:

Morning: /10   Afternoon: /10   Evening: /10

Exercise: Y/N   Details/Activity:

The BEST part of the day was.....

_____

_____

_____

Journal Entry

_____

_____

_____

_____

_____

_____

_____

_____

_____

_____

_____

_____

_____

_____

_____

_____

DAY: M T W T F S S 🦋 DATE_____

(Mood Tracker)

Morning:

Afternoon:

Evening:

Other:

Three words To Describe Today:

1)_____

2)_____

3)_____

🦋 🦋 🦋 🦋 🦋 🦋 🦋

One thing I'm grateful for is:_____

What could have improved today?_____

_____

Three Goals For Tomorrow:

1)_____

2)_____

3)_____

🦋 🦋 🦋 Meals & Snacks 🦋 🦋 🦋

B_____

L_____

D_____

S_____

ENERGY LEVELS:

Morning: /10   Afternoon: /10   Evening: /10

Exercise: Y/N   Details/Activity:

The BEST part of the day was.....

_____

_____

_____

Journal Entry

_____

_____

_____

_____

_____

_____

_____

_____

_____

_____

_____

_____

_____

_____

DAY: M T W T F S S DATE_____

(Mood Tracker)

Morning:

Afternoon:

Evening:

Other:

Three words To Describe Today:

1)_____

2)_____

3)_____

One thing I'm grateful for is:_____

What could have improved today?_____

_____

Three Goals For Tomorrow:

1)_____

2)_____

3)_____

Meals & Snacks

B_____

L_____

D_____

S_____

ENERGY LEVELS:

Morning: /10   Afternoon: /10   Evening: /10

Exercise: Y/N   Details/Activity:

The BEST part of the day was.....

_____

_____

_____

Journal Entry

_____
_____
_____
_____
_____
_____
_____
_____
_____
_____
_____
_____
_____
_____
_____

DAY: M T W T F S S DATE_____

(Mood Tracker)

Morning:

Afternoon:

Evening:

Other:

Three words To Describe Today:

1)_____

2)_____

3)_____

One thing I'm grateful for is:_____

What could have improved today?_____

_____

Three Goals For Tomorrow:

1)_____

2)_____

3)_____

Meals & Snacks

B_____

L_____

D_____

S_____

ENERGY LEVELS:

Morning: /10   Afternoon: /10   Evening: /10

Exercise: Y/N   Details/Activity:

The BEST part of the day was.....

_____

_____

_____

Journal Entry

_____
_____
_____
_____
_____
_____
_____
_____
_____
_____
_____
_____
_____
_____
_____
_____
_____

DAY: M T W T F S S 🦋 DATE _____

(Mood Tracker)

Morning:

Afternoon:

Evening:

Other:

Three words To Describe Today:

1) _____

2) _____

3) _____

🦋   🦋   🦋   🦋   🦋   🦋   🦋

One thing I'm grateful for is: _____

What could have improved today? _____

_____

Three Goals For Tomorrow:

1) _____

2) _____

3) _____

🦋   🦋   🦋   Meals & Snacks   🦋   🦋   🦋

B _____

L _____

D _____

S _____

ENERGY LEVELS:

Morning: /10   Afternoon: /10   Evening: /10

Exercise: Y/N   Details/Activity:

The BEST part of the day was.....

_____

_____

_____

Journal Entry

_____

_____

_____

_____

_____

_____

_____

_____

_____

_____

_____

_____

_____

_____

_____

DAY: M T W T F S S 🦋 DATE_____

(Mood Tracker)

Morning:

Afternoon:

Evening:

Other:

Three words To Describe Today:

1)_____

2)_____

3)_____

🦋　　🦋　　🦋　　🦋　　🦋　　🦋　　🦋

One thing I'm grateful for is:_____

What could have improved today?_____

_____

Three Goals For Tomorrow:

1)_____

2)_____

3)_____

🦋　　🦋　　🦋　　Meals & Snacks　　🦋　　🦋　　🦋

B_____

L_____

D_____

S_____

ENERGY LEVELS:

Morning: /10   Afternoon: /10   Evening: /10

Exercise: Y/N   Details/Activity:

The BEST part of the day was.....

_____

_____

_____

Journal Entry

_____

_____

_____

_____

_____

_____

_____

_____

_____

_____

_____

_____

_____

_____

_____

_____

_____

DAY: M T W T F S S 🦋 DATE _____

(Mood Tracker)

Morning:

Afternoon:

Evening:

Other:

Three words To Describe Today:

1) _____

2) _____

3) _____

🦋 🦋 🦋 🦋 🦋 🦋 🦋

One thing I'm grateful for is: _____

What could have improved today? _____

_____

Three Goals For Tomorrow:

1) _____

2) _____

3) _____

🦋 🦋 🦋 Meals & Snacks 🦋 🦋 🦋

B _____

L _____

D _____

S _____

ENERGY LEVELS:

Morning: /10   Afternoon: /10   Evening: /10

Exercise: Y/N   Details/Activity:

The BEST part of the day was.....

_____

_____

_____

Journal Entry

_____
_____
_____
_____
_____
_____
_____
_____
_____
_____
_____
_____
_____
_____
_____
_____

DAY: M T W T F S S DATE_____

(Mood Tracker)

Morning:

Afternoon:

Evening:

Other:

Three words To Describe Today:

1)_____

2)_____

3)_____

One thing I'm grateful for is:_____

What could have improved today?_____

_____

Three Goals For Tomorrow:

1)_____

2)_____

3)_____

Meals & Snacks

B_____

L_____

D_____

S_____

🦋 🦋 **ENERGY LEVELS:** 🦋 🦋

Morning: /10   Afternoon: /10   Evening: /10

Exercise: Y/N   Details/Activity:

The BEST part of the day was..... ☼

_____

_____

_____

🦋 🦋 Journal Entry 🦋 🦋

_____
_____
_____
_____
_____
_____
_____
_____
_____
_____
_____
_____
_____
_____
_____
_____
_____

DAY: M T W T F S S DATE_____

(Mood Tracker)

Morning:

Afternoon:

Evening:

Other:

Three words To Describe Today:

1)_____

2)_____

3)_____

One thing I'm grateful for is:

What could have improved today?_____

_____

Three Goals For Tomorrow:

1)_____

2)_____

3)_____

Meals & Snacks

B _____

L _____

D _____

S _____

ENERGY LEVELS:

Morning: /10   Afternoon: /10   Evening: /10

Exercise: Y/N   Details/Activity:

The BEST part of the day was.....

_____

_____

_____

Journal Entry

_____

_____

_____

_____

_____

_____

_____

_____

_____

_____

_____

_____

_____

_____

_____

_____

_____

DAY: M T W T F S S 🦋 DATE_____

(Mood Tracker)

Morning:

Afternoon:

Evening:

Other:

Three words To Describe Today:

1)_____

2)_____

3)_____

🦋 🦋 🦋 🦋 🦋 🦋 🦋

One thing I'm grateful for is:_____

What could have improved today?_____

_____

Three Goals For Tomorrow:

1)_____

2)_____

3)_____

🦋 🦋 🦋 Meals & Snacks 🦋 🦋 🦋

B_____

L_____

D_____

S_____

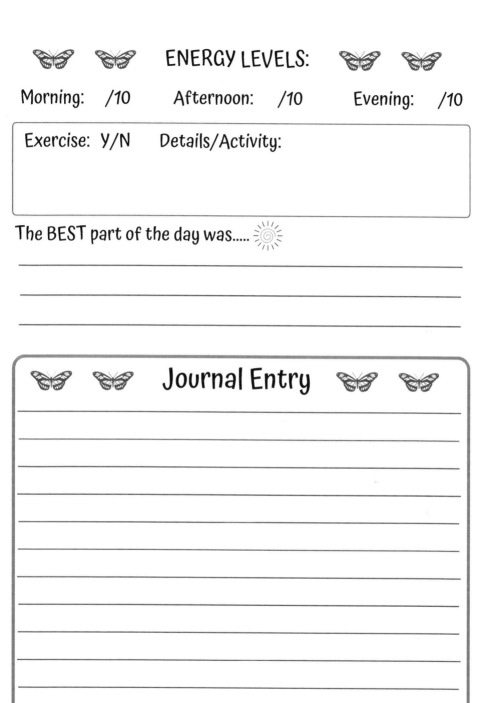

ENERGY LEVELS:

Morning: /10   Afternoon: /10   Evening: /10

Exercise: Y/N   Details/Activity:

The BEST part of the day was.....

_____
_____
_____

Journal Entry

_____
_____
_____
_____
_____
_____
_____
_____
_____
_____
_____
_____
_____
_____
_____
_____

DAY: M T W T F S S 🦋 DATE_____

(Mood Tracker)

Morning:

Afternoon:

Evening:

Other:

Three words To Describe Today:

1)_____

2)_____

3)_____

🦋 🦋 🦋 🦋 🦋 🦋 🦋

One thing I'm grateful for is:_____

What could have improved today?_____

_____

Three Goals For Tomorrow:

1)_____

2)_____

3)_____

🦋 🦋 🦋 Meals & Snacks 🦋 🦋 🦋

B_____

L_____

D_____

S_____

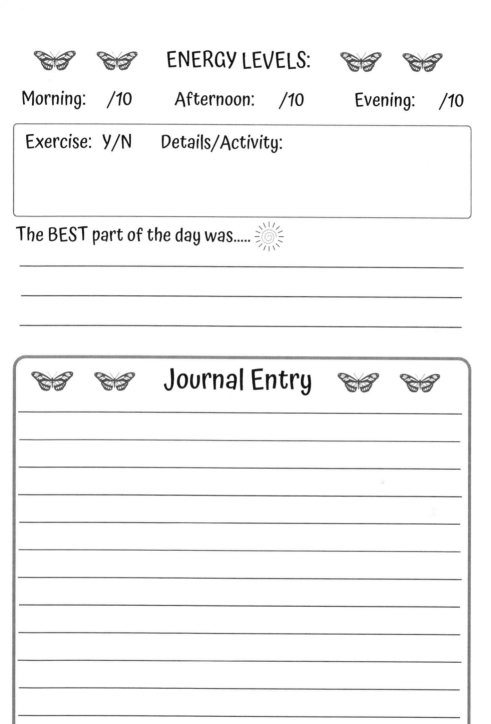

ENERGY LEVELS:

Morning: /10   Afternoon: /10   Evening: /10

Exercise: Y/N   Details/Activity:

The BEST part of the day was.....

_____

_____

_____

Journal Entry

_____
_____
_____
_____
_____
_____
_____
_____
_____
_____
_____
_____
_____
_____
_____
_____
_____

DAY: M T W T F S S   DATE_____

(Mood Tracker)

Morning:

Afternoon:

Evening:

Other:

Three words To Describe Today:

1)_____

2)_____

3)_____

One thing I'm grateful for is:_____

What could have improved today?_____

_____

Three Goals For Tomorrow:

1)_____

2)_____

3)_____

Meals & Snacks

B_____

L_____

D_____

S_____

ENERGY LEVELS:

Morning: /10   Afternoon: /10   Evening: /10

Exercise: Y/N   Details/Activity:

The BEST part of the day was.....

_____

_____

_____

Journal Entry

_____
_____
_____
_____
_____
_____
_____
_____
_____
_____
_____
_____
_____
_____
_____
_____
_____

DAY: M T W T F S S 🦋 DATE_____

(Mood Tracker)

Morning:

Afternoon:

Evening:

Other:

Three words To Describe Today:

1)_____

2)_____

3)_____

🦋　🦋　🦋　🦋　🦋　🦋　🦋

One thing I'm grateful for is:_____

What could have improved today?_____

_____

Three Goals For Tomorrow:

1)_____

2)_____

3)_____

🦋　🦋　🦋　Meals & Snacks　🦋　🦋　🦋

B_____

L_____

D_____

S_____

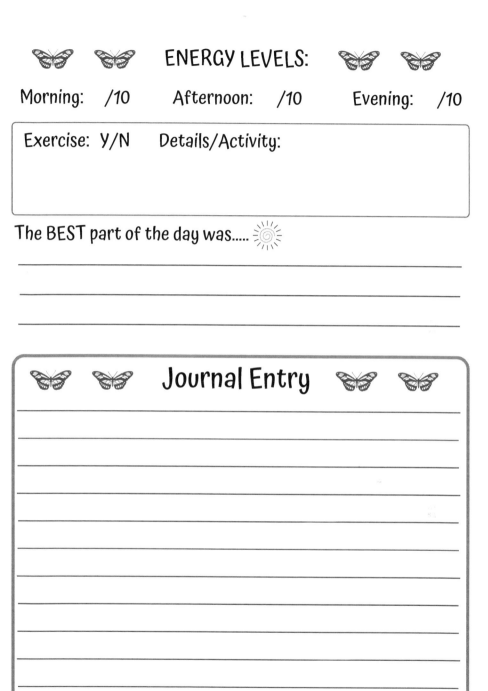

ENERGY LEVELS:

Morning: /10   Afternoon: /10   Evening: /10

Exercise: Y/N   Details/Activity:

The BEST part of the day was.....

_____

_____

_____

Journal Entry

DAY: M T W T F S S 　　　 DATE_____

(Mood Tracker)

Morning: 　　　　　　 Afternoon:

Evening: 　　　　　　 Other:

Three words To Describe Today:

1)_____

2)_____

3)_____

One thing I'm grateful for is:_____

What could have improved today?_____

_____

Three Goals For Tomorrow:

1)_____

2)_____

3)_____

Meals & Snacks

B_____

L_____

D_____

S_____

ENERGY LEVELS:

Morning: /10   Afternoon: /10   Evening: /10

Exercise: Y/N   Details/Activity:

The BEST part of the day was.....

_____

_____

_____

Journal Entry

_____

_____

_____

_____

_____

_____

_____

_____

_____

_____

_____

_____

_____

_____

_____

DAY: M T W T F S S   DATE_____

(Mood Tracker)

Morning:

Afternoon:

Evening:

Other:

Three words To Describe Today:

1)_____

2)_____

3)_____

One thing I'm grateful for is:_____

What could have improved today?_____

_____

Three Goals For Tomorrow:

1)_____

2)_____

3)_____

Meals & Snacks

B_____

L_____

D_____

S_____

ENERGY LEVELS:

Morning: /10   Afternoon: /10   Evening: /10

Exercise: Y/N   Details/Activity:

The BEST part of the day was.....

_____

_____

_____

Journal Entry

_____

_____

_____

_____

_____

_____

_____

_____

_____

_____

_____

_____

_____

_____

_____

_____

_____

DAY: M T W T F S S 🦋 DATE_____

(Mood Tracker)

Morning:

Afternoon:

Evening:

Other:

Three words To Describe Today:

1)_____

2)_____

3)_____

One thing I'm grateful for is:_____

What could have improved today?_____

_____

Three Goals For Tomorrow:

1)_____

2)_____

3)_____

Meals & Snacks

B_____

L_____

D_____

S_____

ENERGY LEVELS:

Morning: /10   Afternoon: /10   Evening: /10

Exercise: Y/N   Details/Activity:

The BEST part of the day was.....

_____

_____

_____

Journal Entry

_____

_____

_____

_____

_____

_____

_____

_____

_____

_____

_____

_____

_____

_____

_____

_____

_____

DAY: M T W T F S S 🦋 DATE_____

(Mood Tracker)

Morning: Afternoon:

Evening: Other:

Three words To Describe Today:

1)_____

2)_____

3)_____

🦋 🦋 🦋 🦋 🦋 🦋 🦋

One thing I'm grateful for is:_____

What could have improved today?_____

_____

Three Goals For Tomorrow:

1)_____

2)_____

3)_____

🦋 🦋 🦋 Meals & Snacks 🦋 🦋 🦋

B_____

L_____

D_____

S_____

ENERGY LEVELS:

Morning: /10   Afternoon: /10   Evening: /10

Exercise: Y/N   Details/Activity:

The BEST part of the day was.....

_____

_____

_____

Journal Entry

_____
_____
_____
_____
_____
_____
_____
_____
_____
_____
_____
_____
_____
_____
_____
_____

DAY: M T W T F S S 🦋 DATE_____

(Mood Tracker)

Morning:

Afternoon:

Evening:

Other:

Three words To Describe Today:

1)_____

2)_____

3)_____

🦋 🦋 🦋 🦋 🦋 🦋 🦋

One thing I'm grateful for is:_____

What could have improved today?_____

_____

Three Goals For Tomorrow:

1)_____

2)_____

3)_____

🦋 🦋 🦋 Meals & Snacks 🦋 🦋 🦋

B_____

L_____

D_____

S_____

ENERGY LEVELS:

Morning: /10   Afternoon: /10   Evening: /10

Exercise: Y/N   Details/Activity:

The BEST part of the day was.....

_____

_____

_____

Journal Entry

_____

_____

_____

_____

_____

_____

_____

_____

_____

_____

_____

_____

_____

_____

_____

DAY: M T W T F S S 🦋 DATE_____

(Mood Tracker)

Morning:

Afternoon:

Evening:

Other:

Three words To Describe Today:

1)_____

2)_____

3)_____

🦋   🦋   🦋   🦋   🦋   🦋   🦋

One thing I'm grateful for is:_____

What could have improved today?_____

_____

Three Goals For Tomorrow:

1)_____

2)_____

3)_____

🦋   🦋   🦋   **Meals & Snacks**   🦋   🦋   🦋

B_____

L_____

D_____

S_____

ENERGY LEVELS:

Morning: /10   Afternoon: /10   Evening: /10

Exercise: Y/N   Details/Activity:

The BEST part of the day was.....

_____

_____

_____

Journal Entry

_____

_____

_____

_____

_____

_____

_____

_____

_____

_____

_____

_____

_____

_____

_____

DAY: M T W T F S S 🦋 DATE_____

(Mood Tracker)

Morning: 😠 🙂 😫 😨 😴

Afternoon: 😠 🙂 😫 😨 😴

Evening: 😠 🙂 😫 😨 😴

Other:

Three words To Describe Today:

1)_____

2)_____

3)_____

🦋 🦋 🦋 🦋 🦋 🦋 🦋

One thing I'm grateful for is:_____

What could have improved today?_____

_____

Three Goals For Tomorrow:

1)_____

2)_____

3)_____

🦋 🦋 🦋 Meals & Snacks 🦋 🦋 🦋

B_____

L_____

D_____

S_____

ENERGY LEVELS:

Morning: /10   Afternoon: /10   Evening: /10

Exercise: Y/N   Details/Activity:

The BEST part of the day was.....

_____

_____

_____

Journal Entry

_____
_____
_____
_____
_____
_____
_____
_____
_____
_____
_____
_____
_____
_____
_____
_____
_____

DAY: M T W T F S S 🦋 DATE_____

(Mood Tracker)

Morning: Afternoon:

Evening: Other:

Three words To Describe Today:

1)_____

2)_____

3)_____

🦋   🦋   🦋   🦋   🦋   🦋   🦋

One thing I'm grateful for is:_____

What could have improved today?_____

_____

Three Goals For Tomorrow:

1)_____

2)_____

3)_____

🦋   🦋   🦋   Meals & Snacks   🦋   🦋   🦋

B_____

L_____

D_____

S_____

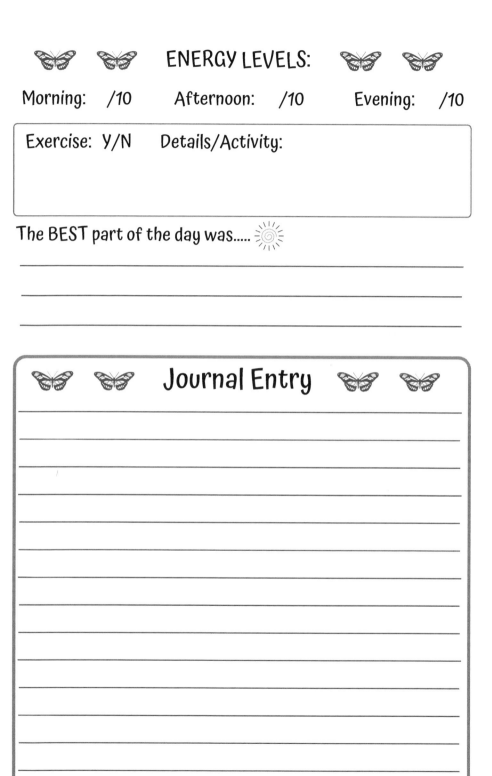

ENERGY LEVELS:

Morning: /10   Afternoon: /10   Evening: /10

Exercise: Y/N   Details/Activity:

The BEST part of the day was.....

Journal Entry

DAY: M T W T F S S 🦋 DATE_____

(Mood Tracker)

Morning: **Afternoon:**

Evening: **Other:**

Three words To Describe Today:

1)_____

2)_____

3)_____

🦋 🦋 🦋 🦋 🦋 🦋 🦋

One thing I'm grateful for is:_____

What could have improved today?_____

_____

Three Goals For Tomorrow:

1)_____

2)_____

3)_____

🦋 🦋 🦋 Meals & Snacks 🦋 🦋 🦋

B _____

L _____

D _____

S _____

ENERGY LEVELS:

Morning: /10   Afternoon: /10   Evening: /10

Exercise: Y/N   Details/Activity:

The BEST part of the day was.....

_____

_____

_____

Journal Entry

_____
_____
_____
_____
_____
_____
_____
_____
_____
_____
_____
_____
_____
_____
_____
_____

DAY: M T W T F S S 🦋 DATE _____

(Mood Tracker)

Morning:

Afternoon:

Evening:

Other:

Three words To Describe Today:

1) _____

2) _____

3) _____

One thing I'm grateful for is: _____

What could have improved today? _____

_____

Three Goals For Tomorrow:

1) _____

2) _____

3) _____

Meals & Snacks

B _____

L _____

D _____

S _____

ENERGY LEVELS:

Morning: /10   Afternoon: /10   Evening: /10

Exercise: Y/N   Details/Activity:

The BEST part of the day was.....

_____

_____

_____

Journal Entry

_____
_____
_____
_____
_____
_____
_____
_____
_____
_____
_____
_____
_____
_____
_____
_____
_____
_____

DAY: M T W T F S S 🦋 DATE_____

(Mood Tracker)

Morning:

Afternoon:

Evening:

Other:

Three words To Describe Today:

1)_____

2)_____

3)_____

🦋 🦋 🦋 🦋 🦋 🦋 🦋

One thing I'm grateful for is:_____

What could have improved today?_____

_____

Three Goals For Tomorrow:

1)_____

2)_____

3)_____

🦋 🦋 🦋 Meals & Snacks 🦋 🦋 🦋

B_____

L_____

D_____

S_____

ENERGY LEVELS:

Morning: /10   Afternoon: /10   Evening: /10

Exercise: Y/N   Details/Activity:

The BEST part of the day was.....

_____

_____

_____

Journal Entry

_____
_____
_____
_____
_____
_____
_____
_____
_____
_____
_____
_____
_____
_____
_____
_____

DAY: M T W T F S S 🦋 DATE_____

(Mood Tracker)

Morning:

Afternoon:

Evening:

Other:

Three words To Describe Today:

1)_____
2)_____
3)_____

🦋   🦋   🦋   🦋   🦋   🦋   🦋

One thing I'm grateful for is:_____

What could have improved today?_____

_____

Three Goals For Tomorrow:

1)_____
2)_____
3)_____

🦋   🦋   🦋   Meals & Snacks   🦋   🦋   🦋

B_____
L_____
D_____
S_____

ENERGY LEVELS:

Morning: /10   Afternoon: /10   Evening: /10

Exercise: Y/N   Details/Activity:

The BEST part of the day was.....

_____

_____

_____

Journal Entry

_____

_____

_____

_____

_____

_____

_____

_____

_____

_____

_____

_____

_____

_____

_____

DAY: M T W T F S S 🦋 DATE_____

(Mood Tracker)

Morning:

Afternoon:

Evening:

Other:

Three words To Describe Today:

1)_____

2)_____

3)_____

🦋   🦋   🦋   🦋   🦋   🦋   🦋

One thing I'm grateful for is:_____

What could have improved today?_____

_____

Three Goals For Tomorrow:

1)_____

2)_____

3)_____

🦋   🦋   🦋   Meals & Snacks   🦋   🦋   🦋

B_____

L_____

D_____

S_____

ENERGY LEVELS:

Morning: /10   Afternoon: /10   Evening: /10

Exercise: Y/N   Details/Activity:

The BEST part of the day was.....

_____

_____

_____

Journal Entry

_____

_____

_____

_____

_____

_____

_____

_____

_____

_____

_____

_____

_____

_____

_____

DAY: M T W T F S S   DATE _____

(Mood Tracker)

Morning:

Afternoon:

Evening:

Other:

Three words To Describe Today:

1) _____

2) _____

3) _____

One thing I'm grateful for is: _____

What could have improved today? _____

_____

Three Goals For Tomorrow:

1) _____

2) _____

3) _____

Meals & Snacks

B _____

L _____

D _____

S _____

ENERGY LEVELS:

Morning: /10   Afternoon: /10   Evening: /10

Exercise: Y/N   Details/Activity:

The BEST part of the day was.....

_____

_____

_____

Journal Entry

_____

_____

_____

_____

_____

_____

_____

_____

_____

_____

_____

_____

_____

_____

DAY: M T W T F S S 🦋 DATE_____

(Mood Tracker)

Morning:

Afternoon:

Evening:

Other:

Three words To Describe Today:

1)_____

2)_____

3)_____

🦋   🦋   🦋   🦋   🦋   🦋   🦋

One thing I'm grateful for is:_____

What could have improved today?_____

_____

Three Goals For Tomorrow:

1)_____

2)_____

3)_____

🦋   🦋   🦋   **Meals & Snacks**   🦋   🦋   🦋

B_____

L_____

D_____

S_____

ENERGY LEVELS:

Morning: /10   Afternoon: /10   Evening: /10

Exercise: Y/N   Details/Activity:

The BEST part of the day was.....

_____

_____

_____

Journal Entry

_____

_____

_____

_____

_____

_____

_____

_____

_____

_____

_____

_____

_____

_____

DAY: M T W T F S S   DATE_____

(Mood Tracker)

Morning: **Afternoon:**

Evening: **Other:**

Three words To Describe Today:

1)_____

2)_____

3)_____

One thing I'm grateful for is:_____

What could have improved today?_____

_____

Three Goals For Tomorrow:

1)_____

2)_____

3)_____

Meals & Snacks

B_____

L_____

D_____

S_____

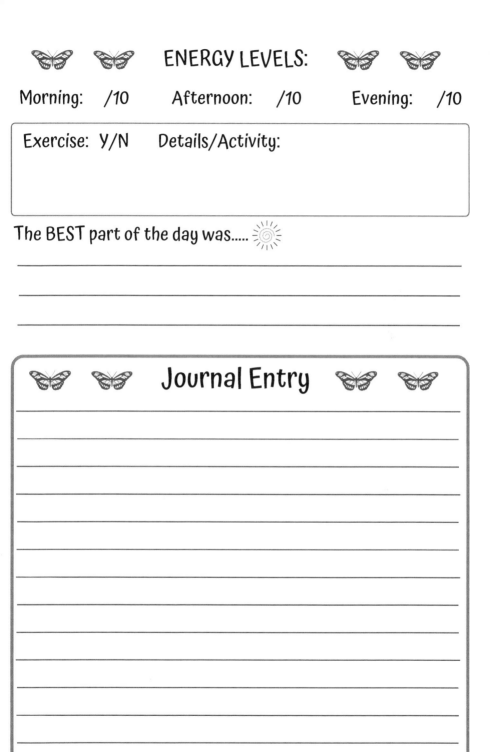

ENERGY LEVELS:

Morning: /10   Afternoon: /10   Evening: /10

Exercise: Y/N   Details/Activity:

The BEST part of the day was.....

_____
_____
_____

Journal Entry

DAY: M T W T F S S   DATE_____

(Mood Tracker)

Morning:

Afternoon:

Evening:

Other:

Three words To Describe Today:

1)_____

2)_____

3)_____

One thing I'm grateful for is:_____

What could have improved today?_____

_____

Three Goals For Tomorrow:

1)_____

2)_____

3)_____

Meals & Snacks

B_____

L_____

D_____

S_____

ENERGY LEVELS:

Morning: /10   Afternoon: /10   Evening: /10

Exercise: Y/N   Details/Activity:

The BEST part of the day was.....

_____

_____

_____

Journal Entry

_____
_____
_____
_____
_____
_____
_____
_____
_____
_____
_____
_____
_____
_____
_____
_____

DAY: M T W T F S S 🦋 DATE_____

(Mood Tracker)

Morning:

Afternoon:

Evening:

Other:

Three words To Describe Today:

1)_____

2)_____

3)_____

🦋 🦋 🦋 🦋 🦋 🦋 🦋

One thing I'm grateful for is:_____

What could have improved today?_____

_____

Three Goals For Tomorrow:

1)_____

2)_____

3)_____

🦋 🦋 🦋 Meals & Snacks 🦋 🦋 🦋

B_____

L_____

D_____

S_____

🦋 🦋 ENERGY LEVELS: 🦋 🦋

Morning: /10   Afternoon: /10   Evening: /10

Exercise: Y/N   Details/Activity:

The BEST part of the day was..... ☀

_____

_____

_____

🦋 🦋 Journal Entry 🦋 🦋

_____
_____
_____
_____
_____
_____
_____
_____
_____
_____
_____
_____
_____
_____
_____
_____
_____

DAY: M T W T F S S DATE_____

(Mood Tracker)

Morning: Afternoon:

Evening: Other:

Three words To Describe Today:

1)_____

2)_____

3)_____

One thing I'm grateful for is:_____

What could have improved today?_____

_____

Three Goals For Tomorrow:

1)_____

2)_____

3)_____

Meals & Snacks

B_____

L_____

D_____

S_____

ENERGY LEVELS:

Morning: /10   Afternoon: /10   Evening: /10

Exercise: Y/N   Details/Activity:

The BEST part of the day was.....

_____
_____
_____

Journal Entry

_____
_____
_____
_____
_____
_____
_____
_____
_____
_____
_____
_____
_____
_____
_____
_____

DAY: M T W T F S S 🦋 DATE_____

(Mood Tracker)

Morning:

Afternoon:

Evening:

Other:

Three words To Describe Today:

1)_____

2)_____

3)_____

🦋 🦋 🦋 🦋 🦋 🦋 🦋

One thing I'm grateful for is:_____

What could have improved today?_____

_____

Three Goals For Tomorrow:

1)_____

2)_____

3)_____

🦋 🦋 🦋 Meals & Snacks 🦋 🦋 🦋

B_____

L_____

D_____

S_____

ENERGY LEVELS:

Morning: /10   Afternoon: /10   Evening: /10

Exercise: Y/N   Details/Activity:

The BEST part of the day was.....

_____

_____

_____

Journal Entry

_____

_____

_____

_____

_____

_____

_____

_____

_____

_____

_____

_____

_____

_____

DAY: M T W T F S S 🦋 DATE_____

(Mood Tracker)

Morning:

Afternoon:

Evening:

Other:

Three words To Describe Today:

1)_____

2)_____

3)_____

🦋 🦋 🦋 🦋 🦋 🦋 🦋

One thing I'm grateful for is:_____

What could have improved today?_____

_____

Three Goals For Tomorrow:

1)_____

2)_____

3)_____

🦋 🦋 🦋 Meals & Snacks 🦋 🦋 🦋

B _____

L _____

D _____

S _____

🦋 🦋 **ENERGY LEVELS:** 🦋 🦋

Morning: /10   Afternoon: /10   Evening: /10

Exercise: Y/N   Details/Activity:

The BEST part of the day was..... ☀

_____

_____

_____

🦋 🦋 ## Journal Entry 🦋 🦋

_____
_____
_____
_____
_____
_____
_____
_____
_____
_____
_____
_____
_____
_____
_____
_____
_____

DAY: M T W T F S S 🦋 DATE _____

(Mood Tracker)

Morning:

Afternoon:

Evening:

Other:

Three words To Describe Today:

1) _____

2) _____

3) _____

🦋   🦋   🦋   🦋   🦋   🦋   🦋

One thing I'm grateful for is: _____

What could have improved today? _____

_____

Three Goals For Tomorrow:

1) _____

2) _____

3) _____

🦋   🦋   🦋   Meals & Snacks   🦋   🦋   🦋

B _____

L _____

D _____

S _____

ENERGY LEVELS:

Morning: /10   Afternoon: /10   Evening: /10

Exercise: Y/N   Details/Activity:

The BEST part of the day was.....

_____

_____

_____

Journal Entry

_____
_____
_____
_____
_____
_____
_____
_____
_____
_____
_____
_____
_____
_____
_____
_____

Printed in Great Britain
by Amazon

67876541R00075